LET'S PLAY
Skating

Aaron Carr

www.av2books.com

FARGO PUBLIC LIBRARY

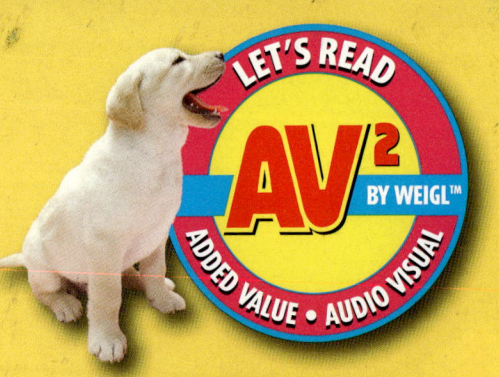

AV² provides enriched content that supplements and complements this book. Weigl's AV² books strive to create inspired learning and engage young minds in a total learning experience.

Your AV² Media Enhanced books come alive with...

Audio
Listen to sections of the book read aloud.

Video
Watch informative video clips.

Embedded Weblinks
Gain additional information for research.

Try This!
Complete activities and hands-on experiments.

Key Words
Study vocabulary, and complete a matching word activity.

Quizzes
Test your knowledge.

Slide Show
View images and captions, and prepare a presentation.

... and much, much more!

Go to www.av2books.com, and enter this book's unique code.

BOOK CODE

J14791

AV² by Weigl brings you media enhanced books that support active learning.

Published by AV² by Weigl
350 5th Avenue, 59th Floor
New York, NY 10118

Website: www.av2books.com   www.weigl.com

Copyright ©2014 AV² by Weigl
All rights reserved. No part of this publication may be reproduced, stored in a retrieval system, or transmitted in any form or by any means, electronic, mechanical, photocopying, recording, or otherwise, without the prior written permission of the publisher.

Library of Congress Control Number: 2013941100
ISBN 978-1-48961-768-2 (hardcover)
ISBN 978-1-48961-769-9 (softcover)

Printed in the United States of America in North Mankato, Minnesota
1 2 3 4 5 6 7 8 9 0 17 16 15 14 13

062013
WEP220513

Project Coordinator: Aaron Carr   Designer: Mandy Christiansen

Weigl acknowledges Getty Images, Dreamstime, Alamy, and Shutterstock as the primary image suppliers for this book. Page 5: Steven G. Johnson.

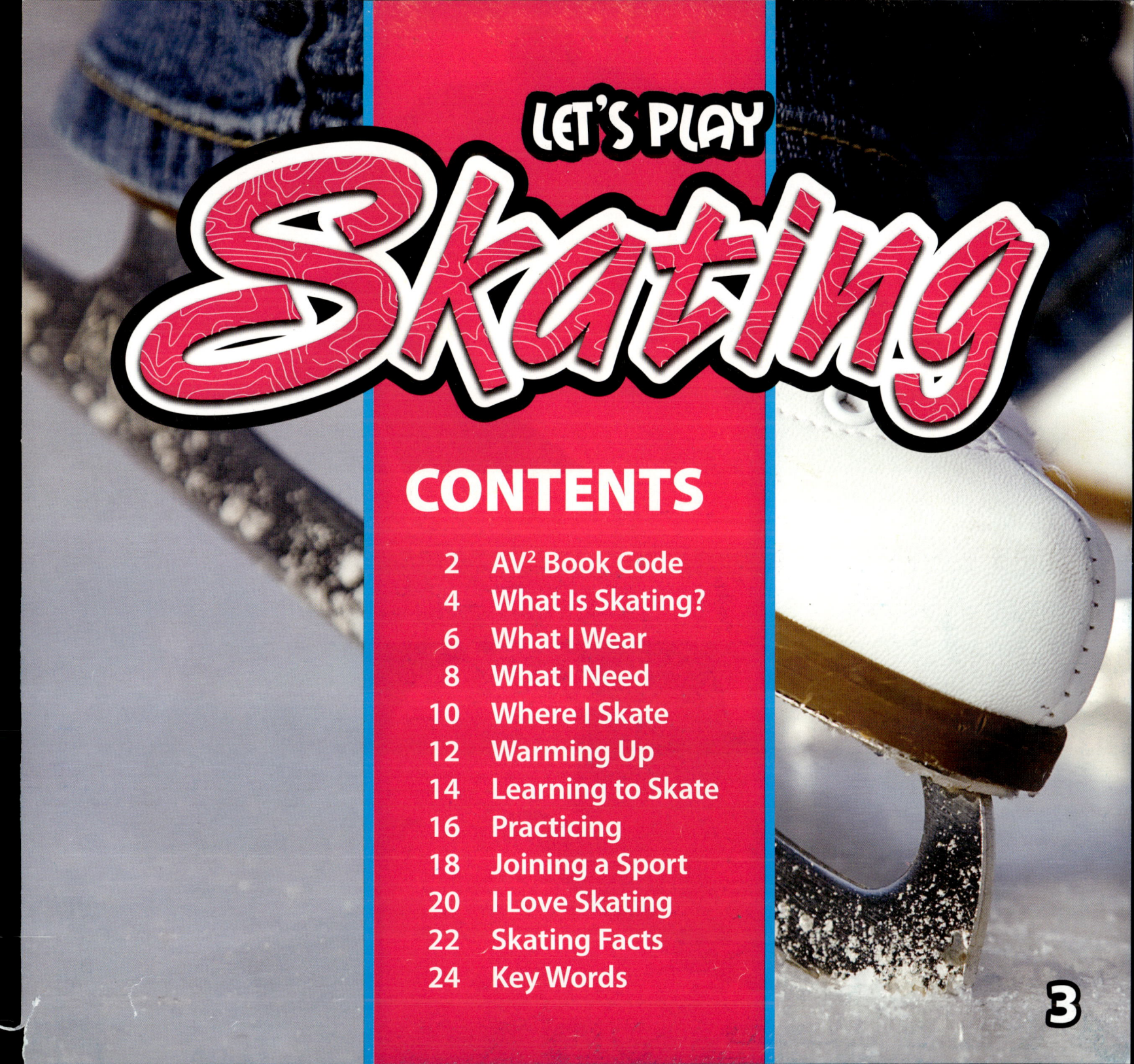

LET'S PLAY Skating

CONTENTS

- 2   AV^2 Book Code
- 4   What Is Skating?
- 6   What I Wear
- 8   What I Need
- 10   Where I Skate
- 12   Warming Up
- 14   Learning to Skate
- 16   Practicing
- 18   Joining a Sport
- 20   I Love Skating
- 22   Skating Facts
- 24   Key Words

I love skating.
I am going skating today.

Skating Fact

The first ice skates were made from animal bones.

5

I get dressed to go skating. I wear warm pants and a winter coat.

Made for Speed

Some skaters wear special skating clothes.

I have my own ice skates.
I wear hockey skates.

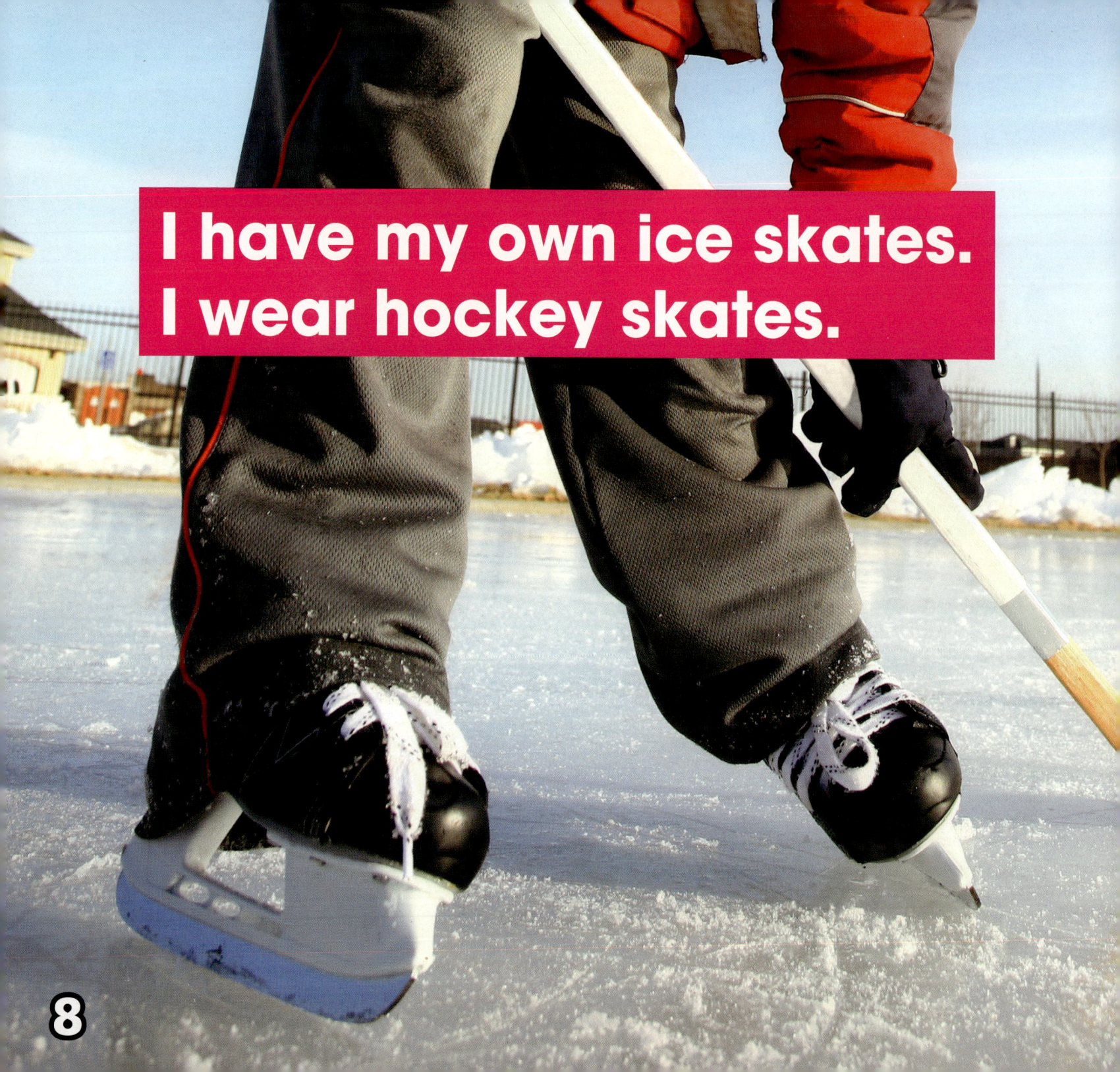

Skating Style

There are different kinds of ice skates.

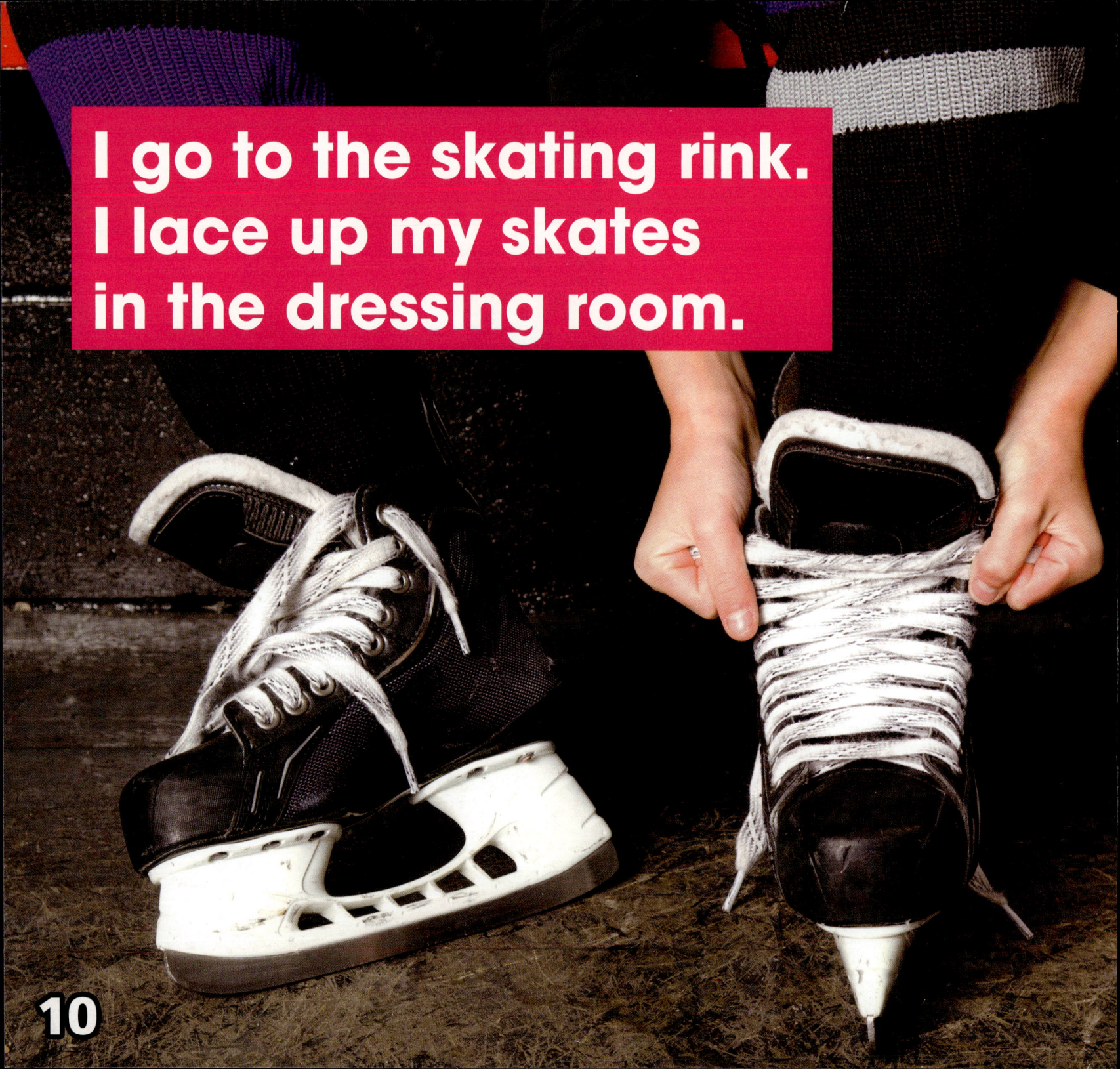

I go to the skating rink. I lace up my skates in the dressing room.

Cleaning Up

The Zamboni cleans the ice.

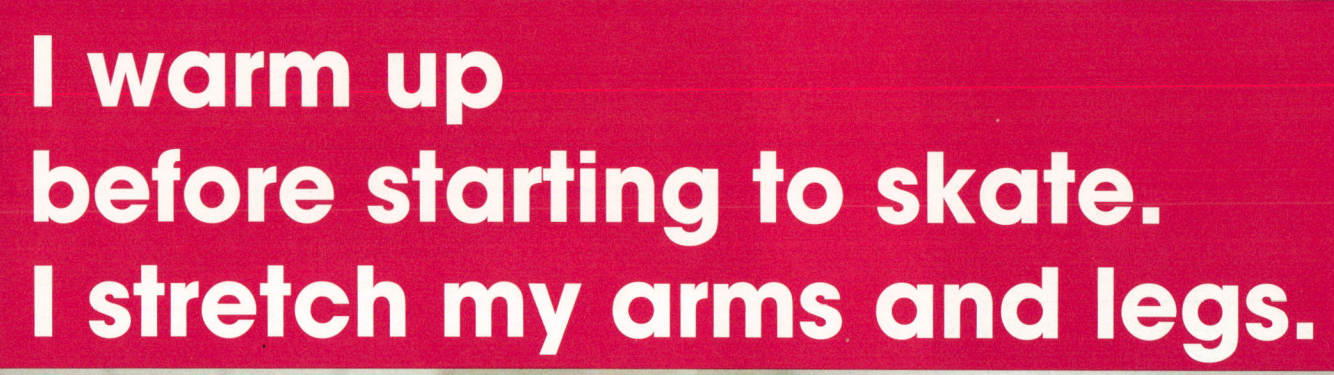

I warm up before starting to skate.
I stretch my arms and legs.

Like a Pro

Skaters often stretch on the ice.

I take skating lessons. I learn how to skate forward and backward.

Skating Skills

There are skating lessons for kids of all ages.

I practice skating on a frozen pond.
I skate around the pond with my friends.

Morning Skate

Pro skaters practice every day.

17

I can play other sports that have ice skating. Hockey, speed skating, and figure skating all use skating.

Let's Dance

Ice dancing is a two-person skating sport.

19

I love skating.

21

SKATING FACTS

These pages provide more detail about the interesting facts found in the book. They are intended to be used by adults as a learning support to help young readers round out their knowledge of each sport featured in the *Let's Play* series.

Pages 4–5

What Is Skating? Skating is an activity and sport that involves sliding on top of ice on ice skates. Ice skates are boots with metal blades attached to the bottoms. Skating began thousands of years ago as a way to travel over ice. The first ice skates had blades made from animal bone. Today, millions of people around the world take part in ice skating, both in indoor rinks and outdoors on frozen lakes, ponds, and rivers.

Pages 6–7

What I Wear Since ice skating takes place in cold environments, skaters usually dress in warm clothing. For outdoor ice skating, it is best to wear snow pants, a winter jacket, gloves, and a hat. Thick, warm socks are also important in order to keep feet and toes warm. Some skaters wear special clothes that are specially designed to be warm while allowing the body to move easily.

Pages 8–9

What I Need Ice skates should fit snugly while allowing enough room for thick socks. As a general rule, a person's skate size should be one size smaller than his or her shoe size. Hockey skates have a smooth, slightly rounded blade. Figure skates have teeth at the toe of each skate, called a toe pick. Speed skates have long blades that extend in front of and behind the boot of the skate.

Pages 10–11

Where I Skate Most people skate at ice rinks. Ice rinks are large buildings with a sheet of artificial ice. Refrigerators keep the building cold to prevent the ice from melting. Ice rinks have dressing rooms where people can sit down while they put on their skates. A machine called an ice resurfacer, or Zamboni, cleans the ice to make it ready for skating. It scrapes off the top layer of the ice and covers it with water, which then freezes to make a smooth, clean surface.

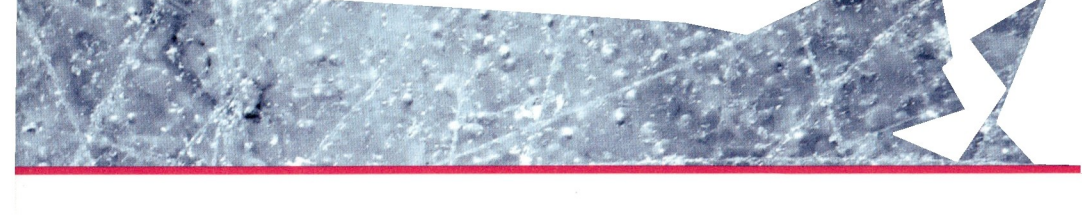

Pages 12–13

Warming Up Doing a proper warm-up helps get the body ready to skate. A good warm-up includes a variety of stretches to loosen up all of the major muscles and reduce the risk of injury. Common stretches to do before ice skating are ankle rolls, side bends, and lunges. Stretching the legs and groin is most important in skating, but it is a good idea to stretch the whole body before any exercise.

Pages 14–15

Learning to Skate Though some kids learn even earlier, most ice skating classes start their beginners classes at 3 years of age. Young skaters start by learning to balance on their skates. Once they can stay balanced, beginning skaters learn to skate frontwards and backwards. As they get better, kids can move up through different levels of skating lessons. Each level expands on skills and helps kids become more confident skaters.

Pages 16–17

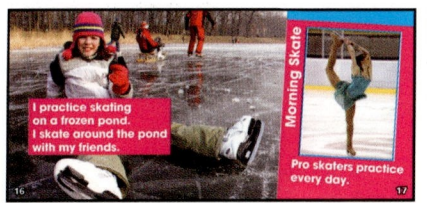

Practicing In cold-weather climates, skating outdoors is one of the most common ways people practice their ice skating skills. However, people need to take extra safety steps when skating outdoors. Before skating on any outdoor ice, it is very important to make sure the ice is safe first. Ice thickness often varies greatly, so it should be tested in more than one place. Also check the color of the ice. Clear blue, black, or green ice is stronger than white or gray ice.

Pages 18–19

Joining a Sport There are several different sports people can go into once they have mastered ice skating. The most common sports that rely on ice skating are hockey, figure skating, speed skating, and ice dancing. These sports use different types of skates with different kinds of blades. Hockey skates are made for speed and maneuverability. Figure skates have toe picks that allow for jumps and tricks. The long blades on speed skates help skaters reach greater speeds.

Pages 20–21

I Love Skating Ice skating is a great way for people to stay active and healthy. Skating is a good form of exercise that relies on speed, strength, and agility. Ice skating promotes physical fitness, cardiovascular health, and balance. However, exercise alone is not enough to stay healthy. In order to get the most out of ice skating, it is important to eat healthful foods. Foods such as fruits, vegetables, and grains give people the energy they need to perform their best.

KEY WORDS

Research has shown that as much as 65 percent of all written material published in English is made up of 300 words. These 300 words cannot be taught using pictures or learned by sounding them out. They must be recognized by sight. This book contains 45 common sight words to help young readers improve their reading fluency and comprehension. This book also teaches young readers several important content words. These words are paired with pictures to aid in learning and improve understanding.

Page	Sight Words First Appearance
4	am, I
5	animal, first, from, made, the, were
6	a, and, get, go, to
7	for, made, some
8	have, my, own
9	are, different, kinds, of, there
10	in, up
12	before
13	like, often, on
14	how, learn, take
15	all
16	around, with
17	day, every
18	can, other, play, that, use
19	is, two

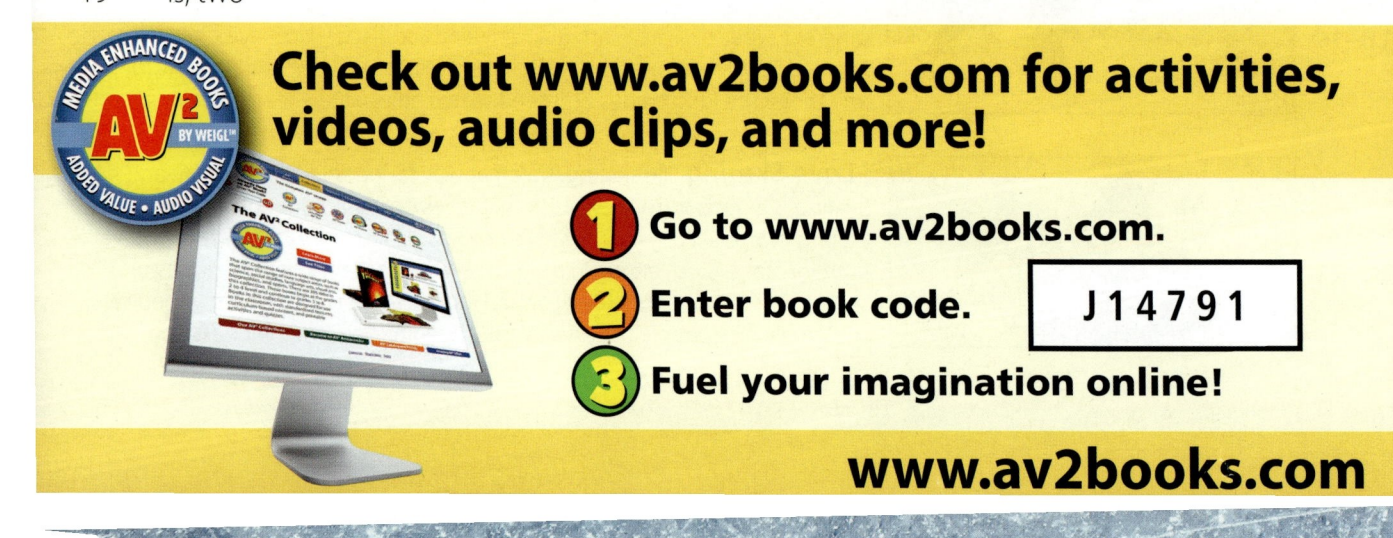

Page	Content Words First Appearance
4	skating, today
5	bones, ice skates
6	coat, pants
7	clothes, skaters
10	dressing room, rink
11	ice, Zamboni
12	arms, legs
13	pro
14	backward, forward, lessons
15	ages, kids, skills
16	friends, pond
17	pro skaters
18	figure skating, hockey, speed skating, sports
19	ice dancing, person

Check out www.av2books.com for activities, videos, audio clips, and more!

1. Go to www.av2books.com.
2. Enter book code. J14791
3. Fuel your imagination online!

www.av2books.com

JAN 2 3 2014